"*SWEET BLOODY SALTY CLEAN* by | ut
the body's canny acclimation to anyth ɘd
eating, self-revulsion, lack of fulfillmen :a-
tions on a few tight contemporary themes, yet I found myself continually surprised by her bluntness and clarity: 'A fly landing in a Venus / flytrap // is getting what it wants / otherwise it wouldn't.' This is a furious text with a keen sense of self; these poems cut."

Niina Pollari
author of *Path of Totality*

"Kritikos writes desire with the precision of Anne Carson, the hunger of Richard Siken, and the stark honesty of Sylvia Plath, but her poetry is all her own. This book is a fleshy, complex reckoning with the impossibility of keeping and the inevitability of losing. Kritikos knows the lengths we will go to in order to feel anything. As alive and essential as pleasure itself."

Lindsay Lerman
author of *I'm From Nowhere* and *What Are You*

SWEET BLOODY SALTY CLEAN

BY

FRANCESCA KRITIKOS

FERAL DOVE BOOKS
MAINE
2023

Would, indeed, anyone be so mad as to declare something his God and, at the same time, eat it?

Cicero, *De Natura Deorum*, 45 BC

I like new things—disposable, new things. I like the way they smell. I throw my possessions in the trash like the ancient Greeks sacrificed meat for the gods, riding that perfect high of catharsis. Whose altar I kneel at I am not yet sure, but I am on my knees.

Milky sake on hotel sheets, a heavy ceramic cup I slipped from the restaurant into my purse like my grandmother would. Thick and weighty in my hand like money. Once you don't have it, you start seeing it everywhere. Glistening purple olives from the country of my people, the slick of oil obscene in my mouth. It's hard to swallow, but I swallow.

Our Western self-imposed famine bores me, that common disease riddling our flesh to nothing, standing in a communion line for cocktails of Adderall and Ozempic, cryo-sculpt and Wegovy. Peanut butter under my acrylic nails, I need to gain ten pounds every winter just to survive. The place I belong is far from here, this land of Benadryl and Senokot, nicotine and levothyroxine, binge and purge, this carceral land of colonizers, cleanses, controlled release.

I dream I am a wooden ship anchored in a harbor, the vessel of me filled with your cum. I speak only the language of steel chains and knotted cords, my palms sliced open just to hold them.

I thought of my beauty as a protective force, but I was wrong.

Spray-tanned skin, French manicure, 23-inch jeans, heels that push me to 5'7," I love only what obstructs me, I fuck only the men who want to watch me starve. I get back from the restroom, I pull out my own chair, I watch you slurp silver oysters and French white wine, I watch you bite the heads off of pale pink shrimp in their delicate fetal curl, I watch you as you ask me if I was throwing up my food, I watch your face slouch with disappointment when I say no.

I buy a sludge made of brown sugar to scrub away my dead skin, I buy organic coconut oil to make my hair soft and smooth, I buy expensive acids to burn myself back to youth, I buy jewel-colored botanical extracts to combat pollutants with an omnipresence comparable only to that of a god's. Everything feels impotent, sur-face-level, another penetrative force trying to change something within me, but I stay the same.

The bathroom I shared with my three siblings growing up was small and dark, the tub dirty and the shower weak, but I fought for it, and I return to it often in my dreams, though I hate these dreams, and I hate that bathroom. Vomit in the trash can, vomit in the sinks, the only way to punish me is to trap me with my own scent.

Going to the store
for calla lilies & 7-up

I believe in beauty
& famine

in my beauty
& my famine

Steel chains for baby
elephants
he told me

Then once it learns
it won't get
free

twine is all
a body needs

In bed I wait
for him
to bring me

three red grapes
on a plate
and fall asleep

Until the day breaks
and the shadows flee

I know that my Redeemer waiteth

In the dark
tongue curled around

my body
like a girl's body

An embrace
is also a reflex
is also a trap

When the stones start to fly
His palms will be empty

This is a prayer

The first rat to get cancer
from Diet Coke

I eat ingredients not meals

Wear my dresses
to sleep

I wash my own feet
now

Waste
through July

On my back

Miss your eyes

I wake up with two new scratches
for each one starting to heal

A message from far away
about changes

to my credit score
Will the payment go through today?

You know I only value austerity
because I value consistency

It's my choice to bleed
onto white sheets

Do I taste the same
as I did last year?

I keep my fruit cold
postponing the loss of money

to maintain liquidity
delay decay

No, I don't kneel
to nature

or pleasure
only simplicity

so if I put up a fight
try again

Like my grandmother
I believe

there is a pill
for everything

You just need to want
to swallow

Boiled potato, cold
and undercooked
with some lettuce
I was petulant

Later I understood
it was all I had
took one bite
ate it slowly

then fast

I don't have to imagine what it's like
to never be alone

I pose for the security cameras
when you're away

I eat quickly, guarding my resources
Later, you'll trick me into thinking

I'm the only one who consumes this way
and I'll believe you forever

Was it Karen Dalton who sang
Take me to your darkest room

Close every window
and lock every door

If there's one thing that will save me
I know this is it

I'm not someone who reads Vogue
but I'm someone who buys Vogue

I believe in sinister conspiracies
but don't think of them often

I dream of animals suffocated in plastic
by my father

I can smell myself right when I wake up
then I don't smell myself anymore

I forget the things I want
so I write them down

I know my fake sugars
I want to outlive everyone thinner than me

No one else but you
has ever called me a good
investment

bought me 00 short shorts
crop tops
drinks

set on fire
everything
I want

We have all the same diseases
We all have the same
disease

You ask me where
I want it
I tell you

Here
is the place
where hunger once reigned

Who's to say what destroyed my life?
Everything is a symptom of something else
Incestuous children of an impotent Father
I learned too late how quick rot spreads
Some organisms are designed to make themselves so soft
They become a threat to themselves
A man has never asked anything of me
Though the meaning shifts as the emphasis does
I, too, have been enormously selfish
On my hungriest days I'll throw everything in the trash
Something is starving the rabbits in this city
I've heard their bones loudening through thin fur
Every night walking home I see them slowly disappear
I can taste our plague in the air

The verb "use" in Greek
is five times as long as it is in English

Consider what has been designed to be optimally
exploited

They say when you buy Nikes
you're buying more than just a sneaker

For animals, where is the line between compulsion
and pleasure?

You believed happiness was relative
and changeable

I knew it had everything to do with satisfaction
which would not be so easily starved

From now on I'll take vitamins
instead of food

If you can't be happy for me, then at least don't leave
me alone

The human state of terror in the face of a need
you can't meet yourself

You're not hungry
until you crave what you hate

The body finds a way
to get three meals a day

You know where to find me

In bed
dripping

with my bandages
loose

If the body was made
for anything

it was emptying

I buy my pears
on credit

Bite them
where they tear

I watch the blood come out
from under my nail

Touch up the polish
darker this time

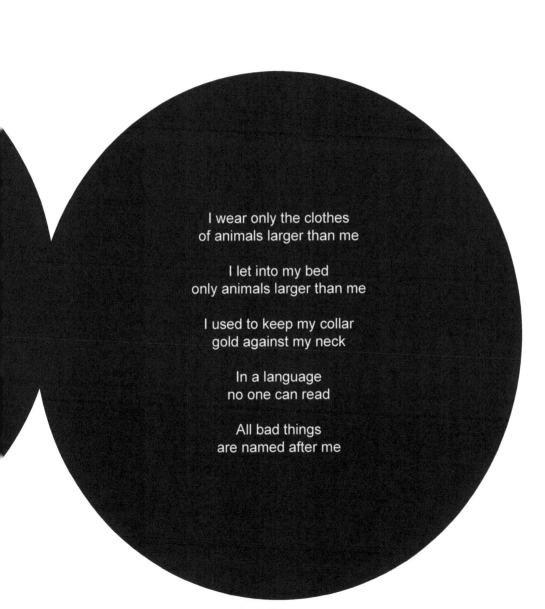

I wear only the clothes
of animals larger than me

I let into my bed
only animals larger than me

I used to keep my collar
gold against my neck

In a language
no one can read

All bad things
are named after me

Who will take out my IUD?

My nails are long
& shiny

but too weak
to scratch with

The thinnest bodies
have never been thinner

The sickest bodies
have never been sicker

I'm easy
to take blood from

I make only
expensive mistakes

I'll kneel
for the bruises

I've never lied
less than this

I no longer worry about who is smarter than me, or more talented. I wonder who is spending their money better than I do. Those are the people I fear.

Caught standing sideways looking at the profile of my body in the mirror. *You used to have an ass*, my sister tells me, then, *Stop looking*.

When I taste a dish that I love, all I can think about is whether I'll be able to recreate it later. I go to the grocery store to try to find the ingredients, or scour the internet. In the next stage, I look for workarounds: I can cut the expensive seeds and avocado, and use mustard and relish instead. I don't need gluten-free flour, I can use the drugstore protein powder I already have in my cabinet. The week goes on, each meal worse than the last.

After dark. You use one shoe to keep the door to your bedroom open. You can afford the things you need but simply choose not to buy them. You let me call my own ride home. You let me pay for it.

I can't afford the things I need, so I buy the things I want. I compulsively Google: "flavor drops" "sugar free flavor drops" "stevia flavor drops" "erythritol flavor drops" "zero calorie flavor drops" "birthday cake flavor drops" "peanut butter flavor drops". The products I want are unavailable, so I pay for the next closest thing, which is to say, that which will never satisfy me.

You ask me how work went today. You care about my employment status, my job stability. You call me sweet, a word no one has ever used to describe me. You're wrong about me, I want to say, before I realize you're just tasting the sucralose coating my tongue.

When I take selfies, I catch myself biting the insides of my cheeks to make my face look thinner. I catch myself posing for photos with my arms unnaturally jutting out, so the flesh isn't pressed against my body, spread.

Sometimes I imagine the outline of your body and wonder what it would be like if I was trapped within it, if I couldn't move beyond its confines. Sometimes I can't stop imagining it.

Rich people can pay to get the fat sucked out of their cheeks, but this causes them to sink in over time, making them look progressively gaunter and gaunter. Rich people can pay to have doctors surgically deliver their babies a month early, allowing them to better preserve their undamaged bodies. Rich people worship at the gold altar of health and, after dark, fuck in the bed of sickness.

The world spins faster, the seasons come quicker. The temperatures get higher, the fires blaze longer. Money doesn't burn anymore, but flesh can still burn. Everything is a deposit or a withdrawal. I can't move the numbers in my account balance, but I learn that I can modify the balance of my body. It can become almost unrecognizable.

If godliness is cleanliness, the Earth has never been so bloody.

"Gluttony and sloth are just the outward manifestations of biochemical perturbations that are going on beneath the surface," a scientist tells the media in a story that is buried as rapidly as it surfaces. Each day my bones feel heavier. Now, when the sun rises, it rises without me. When the sun sets, it doesn't take. I need pills to sleep, and when I accidentally take too many, I hear a woman laughing. In the morning, I drink from a can that promises it will burn my body out of itself, free my flesh from this place.

There is a sentence for everything that is going to happen to me. There is a word for everything I am going to lose.

Senokot
melatonin
vegan omega 3
levothyroxine
probiotic
zinc
vitamin C
acetaminophen
ibuprofen
NyQuil
DayQuil
dark
chocolate
sugar-free
sprinkles
B12
cough
drops
blue
spirulina
CalMag Plus
digestive enzymes
ethinyl estradiol
erythritol
protein powder
fennel seed
bisacodyl 5 mg USP
Please
give it to me
rough

Your body is mine, but I have nothing.
Your game has one rule, and only I know it.
Your cruelty slips into me like something I want.
Your waste is food to someone, don't forget that.
Your tactics don't work on me, I say yes to everything.

You tell me
as I watch you

watch me
trust you

A fly landing in a Venus
flytrap

is getting what it wants
otherwise it wouldn't

Warning on Disease Spread
4 in 10 Struggling Consumers Have Turned to
The Trendy New Anti-Diet Approach to Eating
Designer vagina surgeries double in a year
Food Bills Rise as Inflation Hits Highest Level Since 2008
Eating Disorder Crisis Plaguing
the incarcerated, the imaginary and the dead
Sexual Dysfunction High Among
Americans on Government-Funded Insurance
Women Who Do Not Eat Meat More Likely to Break
Binge-eating during lockdown
The vitamin deficiency affecting 1 in 5
Food Prices Have American Families Sacrificing More
Cancer Cells Most Active During Sleep
New digital tool helps patients manage fear
Why Does My Stomach Hurt?
Friends, I am asking for your prayers
One last time

Always my Keeper
you've taken to following me

upstairs
putting my clothes away

when I don't need them anymore
like God

You see the reason in famine
I do, too

The body never so supple
My body never more yours

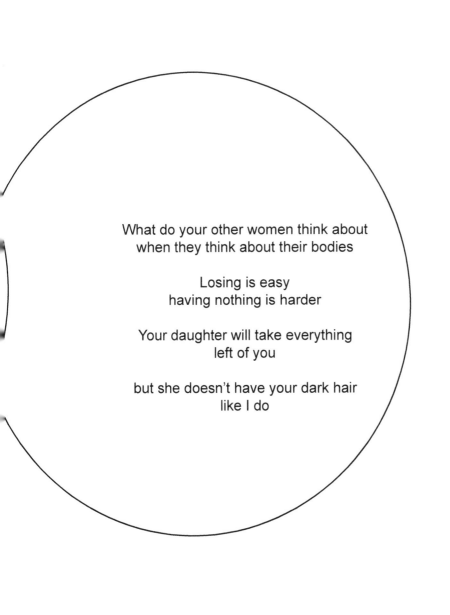

What do your other women think about
when they think about their bodies

Losing is easy
having nothing is harder

Your daughter will take everything
left of you

but she doesn't have your dark hair
like I do

It's 90 degrees
in my apartment

You wouldn't be able to breathe
in here

I can breathe through anything
and have

You tell me this hurts
I'm just waiting

for you
to make me do something

unrecognizable
Every few months

my fig tree sheds all her leaves
Winter can come anytime

and does
I believe

there's no point in saying no
There never has been

Do you think it flatters me, being placed
at the bottom of your list of needs?

You wait for me to smile, placated
by the knowledge that others don't interest you

Why did humans develop preferences?
What advantage does that give?

History has taught us survival lies
in bending over, spreading wide

Welcome to America

Where even the apples
are calorific

And if you see me on the street
I hope I look like shit

Shopping for a new corkscrew
reminds me to masturbate

I like new things
the way they smell

Bestselling
& disposable

Gold
& slippery

Flesh
is currency

Fresh things
turn dirty

Nothing
hurts less

If peaches were diamond
I'd never get wet

I come from people who believe
mirrors are the tools
of the Devil
and here I am

in the bed of a man
who wants only
to suck on a collarbone

I hate mothers
and I love my body

The woman sitting next to me
was crying
I did not turn to face her

A sign reassures me
that in the future I can look like me
only with fewer lines

I love mothers
and I hate my body

No brand
No loyalty

I go to CVS
and Walgreens
interchangeably

I hate mothers
and I hate my body

Vomit in trash cans   sinks
                 your palms
Everything   deserves me

          Should I beg for you?
Bodies aren't that   precious
          but Fake always turns Real

          In the photo of us
       with your arm around me
while I clutch   my purse

          Greed is innate
The body is just   a resource
                 not a home

Daughter   you can fuck
       Consumption   economy
Binge-purge me   Repeat

       Do you know how it feels
when people pray   for the opposite
          of what you want

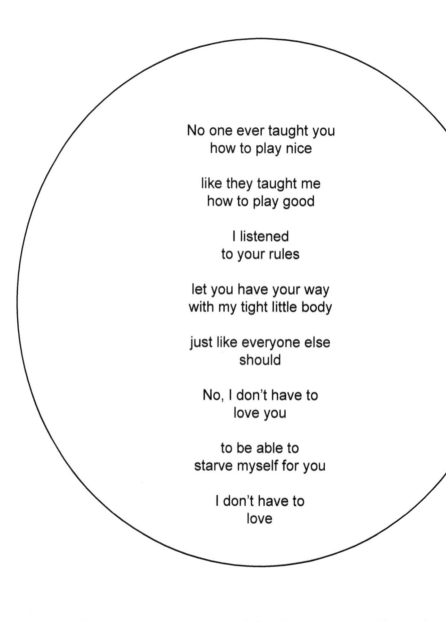

No one ever taught you
how to play nice

like they taught me
how to play good

I listened
to your rules

let you have your way
with my tight little body

just like everyone else
should

No, I don't have to
love you

to be able to
starve myself for you

I don't have to
love

Anything can become
meaning-
less
in the right quantity

Calories

Make-up
samples

I always thought
you deserved

A little bit
of the Truth

I run for the feeling
the day after

One thing leaves my body
another takes its place

It is not in our nature to understand
the difference

Between peace and lethargy
Comfort and sacrilege

If you had me as you wished
I'd be famined

and ridden
to your big bed

No one is good
at ignoring a craving

Though some are better
than others

I take you upstairs
but won't let you stay

Disappointed
when the fruit isn't spoiled

Didn't you know
I wanted to waste you

Plastic is the least
resource-intensive material

I'm not a liar
but I feel like one

Five vibrators under my bed,
three texts from you unread

I don't use things up
before I throw them out

Blue mold on bread,
the bruises on my legs

One hole inside me
dead before you filled it

I'm never not holding
my body
close

Especially when it's
over
yours

I spend you
like
I'm not the currency

Food tastes worse
the more
I eat it

I'm never not taking
the garbage
out

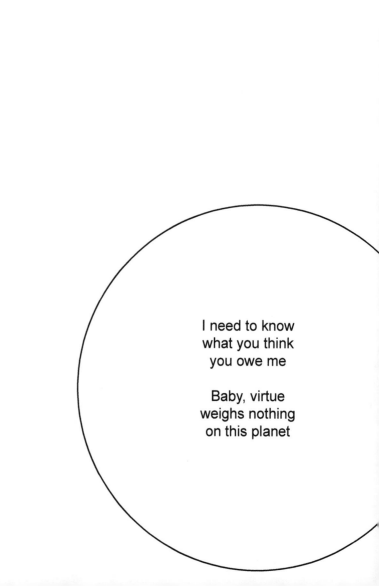

I need to know
what you think
you owe me

Baby, virtue
weighs nothing
on this planet

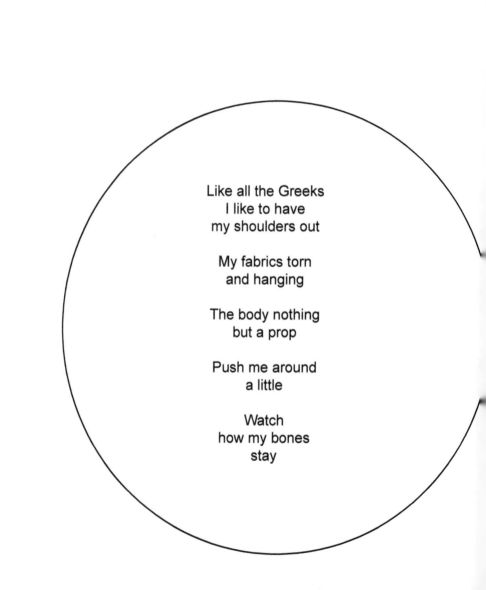

Like all the Greeks
I like to have
my shoulders out

My fabrics torn
and hanging

The body nothing
but a prop

Push me around
a little

Watch
how my bones
stay

In the city
dark like something
crushed

All the men
surrounding me
are cowards

I can tell by the way
I ask them to leave
and they refuse

to fight

Supply
and demand

Benadryl
snack

1200
kcal

aren't you
tired

of the way you're
built

to never stop
wanting

If the world turned
softly

this would be too
easy

I keep drinking glasses of plain almond milk, thick and vanilla, 30 kcal a pop, perfect. Keep getting in bed with my tummy hurting.

I keep going back to get waxed so that when we fuck I can look like a child. I keep my eyes on the ceiling as the black wax burns against my skin, not interested in seeing what my body wants for me. I keep buying wax passes for discounts on Brazilians. They tell me it's $150 upfront, and I have to sign and initial a bunch of papers, a taking on of responsibility that possibly negates the part where I look like a child. I keep my card on file, the Mastercard ending with 1883? Yes, I keep saying.

I keep the receipt from the wax salon, which says $402, $301.50 and $100.50 in different spots, but I don't see $150 anywhere. None of the numbers seem to have any connection, though I know that can't be true. I don't check my bank account, don't want to know how the math adds up, breaks down.

I keep walking to the drugstore for vanilla protein powder and Gatorade Zero, the light blue one. I keep being unable to resist the indigestibility of inulin, the protein powder's key ingredient. Inulin may cause bloating and weight loss, it sits in the intestines and fills them up. One day I accidentally buy the dark blue shade of Gatorade Zero, and when I realize, something like anger tries to move inside of me but lacks the space.

I keep remembering my father's anger, like a full glass of wrong-colored liquid in a raised hand, dropping. I'd have it, too, if I let myself. I think you have it, but I don't have the proof. We keep playing nice with each other, all stones left unturned, unthrown. You are too smart to let me see your anger, knowing it is the only thing that may rouse me to move in a direction away from you, and it is to your advantage that I stay in your big bed where you knot up my hair and talk onto the silence.

I keep getting sleep paralysis, feeling the demonic presence of a masculine entity on my chest. The men who get on top of me don't tend to carry their own weight. Keep letting it drop.

I keep meaning to squeeze your head when it's between my thighs, but I can't bring myself to the action. When we meet at the wine bar by your apartment I mean to tell you that we shouldn't be doing this anymore, that there is every reason we should not be in bed together, but I haven't eaten enough, and I'm too tired to say words that I don't believe, or words that I do.

I keep ignoring your texts, or trying to. You keep up the silence, until I start seeing you behind the wheel of every car. Until I start soaking through my underwear and clothes, starving. You tend toward the dark, and I am looking for the light: We keep ending up in the same place. You feed me through the right mouth, and I keep trying to make it last. I keep trying to make it the last time. I stumble home, from dark to dark.

I keep bleeding. Eight months I didn't get my period and felt like a god. I let anyone have me, wanted to see who would try. I fucked my idols until they weren't my idols. Now I have my period again, and I understand the freedom was never real: I'll let anyone have me. I fuck my idols until they aren't my idols, but I just want them back.

I keep using my wand vibrator while watching videos of fully clothed women speaking softly, the only time sex feels safe. Keep falling asleep with the bulb filling the gap between my thighs like an egg. Perfect things have nothing alive in them, I keep noticing.

Bent over
You refuse to see me
As anything but
What you need
It makes it so
Nothing else exists
I dream of sterility
It's better
For both of us
When we face each other
One of us is just
A resource to be managed
I have never been more
In love

Every purchase serves
the same economy
e.g. I see you
even when I'm not
seeing you

Nothing alive
is clean

I wish that wasn't
the truth

I'm on my knees
in my dreams

Like my mother
and my mother's mother

Scrubbing
tile floors

My tastes are beige
but

I'm wearing that neon
pink bra

The one you gave me
right before

you came
all over it

My sickness
isn't worse
than anyone else's

but I'm too dark
to turn
blonde

There's more shame
in asking for the thing you want
than there is in taking it

e.g. the way I used to
bleed
which was only by force

It's true, once you fill a hole
its shape will change
to outsmart you

Now I'd rather have the sun
in my eyes
than yours on my back

I'd like to be
hard to find
in a wide open space

I only search for what I know
I won't find

Wash my hands
then drink the water

I used to watch my body
beneath tires

My meat wants so badly
to be warm

It burns
itself

I loved you for ten years
then stopped

You spoke of taking me
far away from here

Fucking me
for days

My Greek skin
in your teeth

My Anatolian blood
on your tongue

The pleasure was mine
according to your scriptures

I watched you knot the locks
of your quietest child

Snake smaller than its prey
Pig smarter than its slaughterer

Frothing at the seams
means lust or disease

Praying
every night
for this
to get harder

Believing
in the creature
you've made
of my body

Hungry

To be loved means to be stripped
clean

under your mouth
under your hands

in my bed
in my apartment

in our mutation
in the history of our Earth

There aren't enough people in this city
to hide my body
from you

I try to surround myself with things
that bite

I can only swallow
in the Free World

where everything is sharp
and getting sharper

We've never been this hungry
or close
to extinction

Eating too much
after periods of restriction
is the body's completely natural response

Overeating after periods of starvation
is a perfectly normal reaction
of the body

Heightened eating post-starvation
is a wholly natural aftereffect
in the animal body

After starvation, overeating is the
absolutely normal answer
of the organism

Hyperfeeding in the seasons after starvation
is the body's consummately physiological
anti-action

In the afterhunger, ultraconsuming
is a totally natural counteraction
for the living occurrence

Post-famine gorging
is an utterly typical act
for the organ-cluster

My shepherd,
Those who come before us
are only our teachers
if we let them

I wanted to tell you,
my shepherd, how

It is possible not to feel anything
for a while
But you
already knew

How is it possible,
my shepherd

Every year
I make less money

Have you eaten
your eggs today,
my shepherd?
Your meat?

There have been other men,
shepherd,
but none whom I regret
not having spent his life with
more than you

Who taught me
for what
my body is a sleeve

Fresh figs
Bacon
Bag of pretzels
Bar of sage soap

Sweet
Bloody
Salty
Clean

At the end of a fast
there is nothing
a body won't take

Walking past the church it's the trash on the steps I notice. I think, *I want to give myself to you.* It's true, I placed myself before you like that once. In ancient Greece, "parasite" meant "priest." Maybe that's why I let you root in me, teeth and nails and fingers and cock. Maybe I thought that by taking of me, you'd make me better. Lead me not into temptation. Lead me from this place into heaven. You loved me best at my frailest, when eating meant straddling your lap, spitting wine in your mouth. A handful of supplements and my baby pink pill. When you couldn't be with me, I pressed play on the recording of your voice and opened my mouth.

God's plan was austerity,
locusts and wild honey.

The bruises on my thigh shaped like your hand, an infection spreading its tendrils, blooming nightshade breathing out poison like love. The bruise on my neck shaped like your arms and like gravity and like silence. The bruise on my cheekbone, a gift from myself. Bruises on my calves like my bones knowing better, reaching away from here.

Now my knees bruise each other,
the only kiss I'll know forever.

I struggle to separate my feelings from the pharmaceuticals teething their way through my abdomen. The generic version of life, cheaper and contaminated, but the active ingredients are the same, similar enough, and the side effects come as expected, in waves, in bodies thrust against the rocks. The point of medicating is to be OK with anything. I believe in the cause. I don't lie anymore because everything is true. Ask me any question and the answer is yes.

A parasite can't die: when it bleeds, it bleeds its host.
Does that mean you'll own me forever?

A successful infection must end with the death of the host. In consuming, what the parasite really wanted was to starve. To be overtaken by infection, the body must decide to surrender. But I keep surviving. And survival is the opposite of pleasure. And love is the only sickness I'll never know.

How long would it take you to find $35 worth of products you want?

Can you freeze bananas in their wrappers, I mean skins?

I can't afford some of the things I want and I call it having morals.

I can't afford some of the things I don't want and I call it having morals.

The dress looks good on me the way everything does. You look good on me the way everyone does.

The opposite is also true.

There's a lesson in celibacy if you're someone like me.

After eating, my dog takes the blanket between his teeth and growls. Is it violence that's missing?

I can tell when I'm full, but I can't tell if I like what's filling me.

I can tell when I'm empty, and I don't have to decide whether I like it or not.

The period of time between my nails being too short and too long is not discernible.

Four days for a scab to heal.

Who decides how much of an ingredient makes a meal?

If you hate what you eat you'll grow to love it.

The opposite is also true.

There's a lesson in celibacy if you're someone who craves things because they crave you.

I don't trust anything that returns to where it came from.

What other animals sleep next to mirrors? Watch their parents grow old?

Violence hides best in the familiar. Flesh gripping flesh bleached into deli meat, leather purse, nylon.

Food for the bugs.

Bites on my legs, gifts I get to open later.

I get to open my mouth later.

Tonight I stained my white dress. Tonight was an event.

A selection of these poems have been published by Pitymilk Press as a limited-edition chapbook with artwork, titled *In the Bed of Sickness*. Thank you to Pitymilk Press for supporting my work.

Francesca Kritikos is a Greek-American writer based in Chicago. She is the editor in chief of SARKA, a journal and publisher focused on works of the flesh.

@fmkrit
bio.site/fmkrit
sarkapublishing.com

PUBLISHED BY FERAL DOVE BOOKS

ISBN 979-8-9856764-8-8

Thank you for being here.
Thanks to Kaisa Saarinen for editing assistance.
Book design by Evan Femino.

feraldove.com

Printed in the USA
CPSIA information can be obtained
at www.ICGtesting.com
JSHW070043150624
64779JS00007B/55